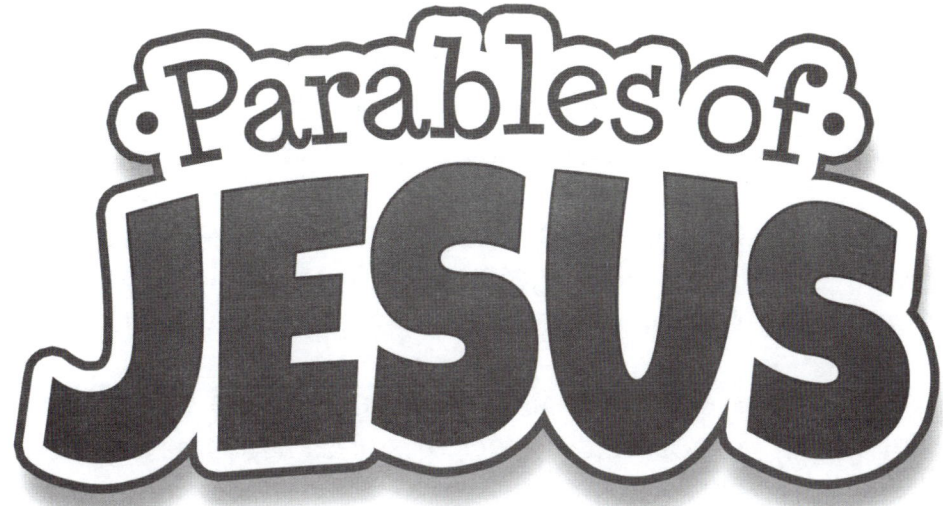

Coloring & Activity Book

Written by Linda Tucker-Bays

Illustrated by Karen Jones

Scripture marked (NIV) taken from the HOLY BIBLE, NEW INTERNATIONAL VERSION ®. NIV®. Copyright © 1973, 1978, 1984, 2011 by Biblica, Inc.®. Used by permission. All rights reserved worldwide.

Scripture marked (NCV) taken from The Holy Bible, New Century Version®. Copyright © 2005 by Thomas Nelson, Inc.

The purchase of this activity book grants you the rights to photocopy the contents for classroom use.
Notice: It is unlawful to copy these pages for resale purposes. Copy permission is for private use only.

Copyright © 2017 Warner Press, Inc. All rights reserved. Made in USA

305800211014

The Forgiving Moneylender
(Luke 7:36-50)

One evening, a Pharisee named Simon invited Jesus for dinner. While He was there, a woman began to cry, wash Jesus' feet with her tears, dry them with her hair, and pour perfume on them. Simon knew she had lived a sinful life, and he did not like to see her shocking behavior in his house! When he complained to Jesus about it, Jesus told him this short story.

Two people owed money to a moneylender. One owed 50 days wages, and the other owed 500 days wages. They didn't have enough to repay him, so he forgave them both. They never had to pay him back!

Then Jesus asked Simon, "Which of these two people would love the moneylender more?" Simon answered, "I guess the one who owed more money would love him more."

Simon answered correctly, but he didn't understand that Jesus could forgive sins. Not only did He forgive the woman, but He could also forgive Simon! The woman knew she had been forgiven for all of her sins, and she loved Jesus more. She loved Jesus so much that she let him know it.

© 2017 Warner Press, Inc All rights reserved   E4793

Use the code to find out what Jesus said to the woman.

A - 1	N - 14
B - 2	O - 15
C - 3	P - 16
D - 4	Q - 17
E - 5	R - 18
F - 6	S - 19
G - 7	T - 20
H - 8	U - 21
I - 9	V - 22
J - 10	W - 23
K - 11	X - 24
L - 12	Y - 25
M - 13	Z - 26

__ __ __ __ __ __ __ __ __ __ __ __ __ __ __ __ __ __ __ .
25 15 21 18 19 9 14 19 1 18 5 6 15 18 7 9 22 5 14

__ __ __ __ __ __ __ __ __ __ __ __ __ __ __ __ __ __ __ __ .
25 15 21 18 6 1 9 20 8 8 1 19 19 1 22 5 4 25 15 21

__ __ __ __ __ __ __ __ __ ! Luke 7:48, 50 (NIV)
7 15 9 14 16 5 1 3 5

© 2017 Warner Press, Inc All rights reserved   E4793

The Unmerciful Servant
(Matthew 18:21-35)

Jesus told the story of a king who wanted to collect all of the money that his servants owed him. One man, who owed him millions of dollars, begged the king to be patient with him and promised that he would one day repay the king. The king felt sorry for him, canceled the debt, and let him go. Soon after this, the servant saw a man who owed him a much smaller amount of money. He grabbed the man, began to choke him, and demanded that the man pay him back. Just like the first servant, this man begged the servant to be patient and promised that he would one day pay him back. But the servant refused and had the man thrown into prison. When others learned that this happened, they were very upset and complained to the king. The king was very angry that this servant received mercy and didn't show it to another. The king ordered the servant to jail to be tortured until he could pay back all that he owed.

Jesus died on the cross for us so we can be forgiven. He wants us to forgive others too!

Find the message below by crossing out the all of the As, Qs, and Ms and writing all of the remaining letters in the spaces.

__ __   __ __ __ __   __ __ __   __ __

__ __ __ __ __ __ __ __   __ __ __ __ __ __!

The Rich Young Fool
(Luke 12:13-31)

One day Jesus was teaching His disciples in the middle of a huge crowd. While He was teaching, someone in the crowd called out, "Teacher, tell my brother to divide the family inheritance with me!" Jesus first warned the people that being greedy is dangerous and then told a story.

He said there was a rich man who produced a very good crop one year. He didn't have enough room to store the entire crop, but he wanted to keep it anyway. He tore down his barn and built bigger barns so he could store it all. This way he would no longer have to do any work. But God called him a fool for doing so much to store what he didn't need because he was going to die that night. He would not get to enjoy anything he had prepared for himself. He should have spent more time learning about God and getting ready for heaven.

Jesus finished by saying, "This is how it will be with anyone who stores up things for himself but is not rich toward God" (from Luke 12:21, NIV).

Find the words of this quote in the puzzle below:

```
D C R C C P O W B H S Z P
H R O Q L Q W Z W N F U H
K B A I S H T K S I H T S
E T G W O T H E Y K L C N
F N I G O F U J B U R L H
U O O L H T B F T C Y V E
D O C Y F E J L H H B W W
B Z V S N U S E I U C O K
T I G T N A I S N M P I E
L M F O U R S M G L K H R
F V O R L B J I S G T T W
Y X R E N B U H Q O Z I O
D V S S Z R E T N D T W H
```

The Widow and the Unjust Judge
(Luke 18:1-8)

Jesus told this story to help people know to keep praying and not give up.

There was a widow who had been treated unfairly, so she went to a judge for help. This judge wasn't nice to God or to people, and he didn't want to help her. She kept coming to him anyway, and finally he decided to help her so that she would quit bothering him.

Jesus said that God is very different from this judge. He has chosen us! God loves us and wants to help us. He wants us to pray and to keep praying. God wants us to have faith!

After telling this story, Jesus asks a question that He wants His disciples to think about. To find out what the question is, arrange the letters below each column in the table to form the question. The first column is done for you.

W				■					
F				■					
O		■						?	■

```
F   N   L   E   A   J   T   I   U   H
O   I   N   D   R   A   S   T   S   S
W   I   L   L   F   E   H       H
```

From Luke 18:8 (NIV)

Answer: WHEN THE SON OF MAN COMES, WILL HE FIND FAITH ON EARTH?

The Birds and the Lilies
(Matthew 6:25-34)

Jesus knew that when people worry about things, it distracts them and keeps them from being the best followers of Jesus that they can be. He told His followers these two very short parables to help them stop worrying:

Think about the birds. The birds don't waste their energy planting crops and storing them for later so they will be able to eat. God will make sure they have food because He cares for them.

Now think about the lilies. The lilies don't work hard to have beautiful flowers. God makes them even more beautiful than the richest person's clothing!

Jesus reminded the people that God cares about them much more than He cares about birds and flowers. God doesn't want any of us to waste our energy worrying about things like food, money, and clothing. He wants us to know that He'll take care of us. When we don't waste our energy worrying, we have more energy to be like Jesus and help others know about Him. That's what we're here for!

Use the clues to find the code for the verse below.

CLUES:

A place to take a bath: __ __ __
                                    1 2 3

An animal you can ride: __ __ __ __ __
                               4 5 6 7 8

Another word for angry: __ __ __
                             9 10 11

The opposite of empty: __ __ __ __
                        12 2 13 13

An item used to open a lock: __ __ __
                                14 8 15

A part of a bird or an airplane: __ __ __ __
                                  16 17 18 19

VERSE:

__ __ __ __ __ __ __ __ __ __ __ __ __ __ __ __ __ __ __ __ ,
7 8 8 14   12 17 6 7 1   19 5 11 7   14 17 18 19 11 5 9

__ __ __ __ __ __ __ __ __ __ __ __ __ __ __. __ __ __ __
10 18 11   16 4 10 1   19 5 11   16 10 18 1 7   1 4 8 18

__ __ __ __ __ __ __ __ __ __ __ __ __ __ __ __ __ __ __ __ __
10 13 13   15 5 2 6   5 1 4 8 6   18 8 11 7   16 17 13 13

__ __ __ __ __ __ __ __ __ __ __ __. __ __ __ __ __ __ __ 6:33 (NCV)
3 8   9 8 1   10 7   16 8 13 13   9 10 1 1 4 8 16

© 2017 Warner Press, Inc All rights reserved   E4793

The Lost Sheep
(Luke 15:1-7)

The tax collectors and sinners started to gather around Jesus to hear what He had to say. The Pharisees and scribes didn't think it was right to hang out with such people! They started to complain about it, and Jesus told them this story:

If a man owns a hundred sheep and one of them gets lost, of course he would leave the ninety-nine safe sheep to go find the lost one. Once he found it, he would carefully bring it home and then call all of his friends and neighbors to join him in a celebration that the lost sheep had been found.

Jesus told this and other stories about lost things to help the people understand that He wants even the sinners and tax collectors to be part of His family. He loves them and celebrates when one of them begins to follow Him.

Jesus needs our help to tell people about His love so that they won't be "lost" like the sheep.

Help the shepherd find his lost sheep.

The Wedding Feast and the Banquet
(Luke 14:7-24)

One day Jesus was eating at the house of a ruler of the Pharisees. He noticed that people were taking places of honor for themselves, so He told the story of a wedding feast. He warned His listeners that if they took a place of honor at the wedding feast, the host would come and tell them that they were in the wrong place. This would be embarrassing. Instead, Jesus told them to take the lowest place. Then the host would tell them to move up to a higher place. This would bring them honor.

Next, Jesus told the host that when he gives a banquet, it's better to invite those who can't repay him because it's better to be repaid by God. Someone heard that and said, "Blessed are the people who will share a meal in God's Kingdom." Jesus told one more story about a man who invited many people to a banquet. When it was time, all of the invited people gave excuses and did not come. The man told his servant to go out quickly to bring in the poor people and people with disabilities to enjoy the banquet. When he realized that he still had room for more people, he told the servant to go search everywhere and urge people to come. The people who were originally invited missed out!

Jesus would like for all people to be part of His kingdom, but some people choose to miss out.

Use the clues to fill in the correct letters in the puzzle below.

1. The second letter of the alphabet
2. The letter between G and I
3. Two letters after H
4. The letter before D
5. The fourth vowel
6. Three letters after B
7. The letter between T and V
8. Two letters after J
9. Three letters before P
10. Three letters after P

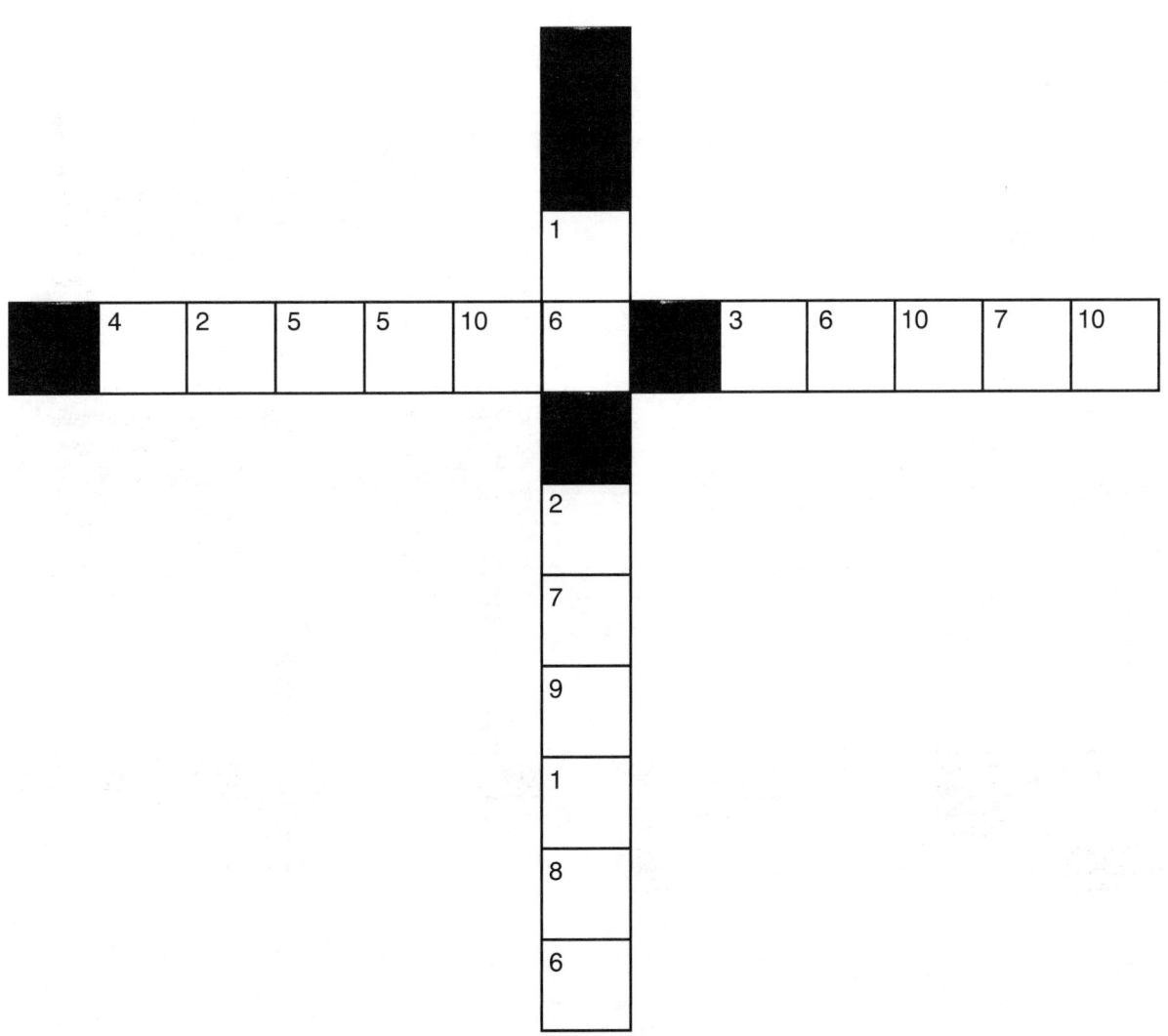

© 2017 Warner Press, Inc All rights reserved   E4793

ANSWERS

Page 3

Your sins are forgiven. Your faith has saved you. Go in peace!

Page 5

We honor God by forgiving others!

Page 7

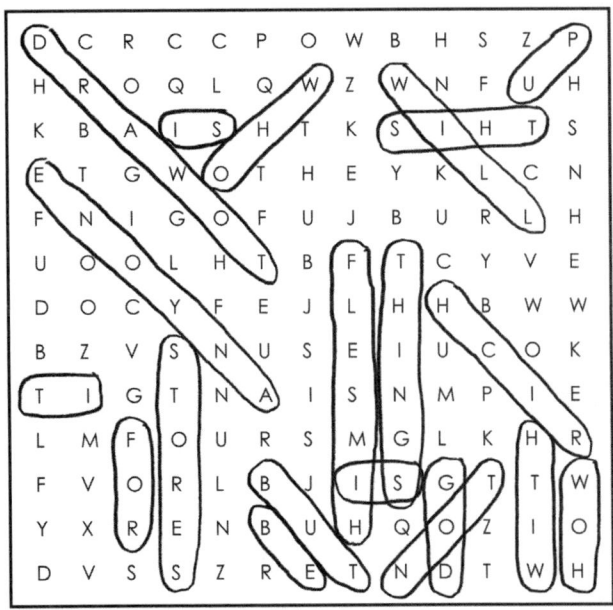

Page 9

WILL JESUS FIND FAITH ON EARTH?

Page 11

CLUES:
TUB
HORSE
MAD
FULL
KEY
WING

VERSE:
Seek first God's kingdom and what God wants. Then all your other needs will be met as well.
Matt. 6:33 (NCV)

Page 13

Page 15

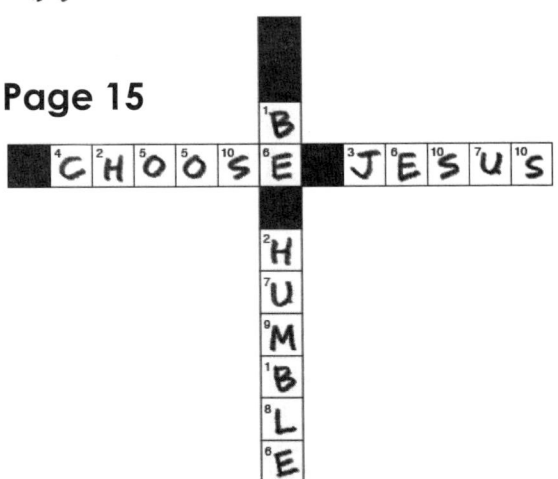

CHOOSE JESUS'S HUMBLE

© 2017 Warner Press, Inc All rights reserved E4793